Selected Works

# CORNELIUS GURLITT

## Piano Solos by
## Master Composers of the Period

Editor: Dale Tucker
Art Design: Joann Carrera
Artwork Reproduced on Cover: *Old English Cottage* by Benjamin Williams Leader

W9-AZV-109

# CORNELIUS GURLITT

**Born: February 10, 1820, Germany**
**Died: June 17, 1901, Germany**

Cornelius Gurlitt was born into an artistic family in Altona, Germany, February 10, 1820. His brother, Louis, was a renowned artist, recognized for his paintings of landscapes. Later, family members became respected musicians, composers, and one a conductor. Gurlitt studied piano with Reinecke and then moved to Copenhagen, Denmark, to study with Weyse. He met Schumann, Franz, and other composers during a concert tour of Europe in 1845. Each had an influence on his writing style thereafter, and he is best remembered for these piano pieces. In addition to his piano works, Gurlitt also composed numerous works for stringed instruments, song cycles, and two operas.

Gurlitt was also a fine organist, and in 1864 was appointed as organist to the Altona Cathedral, where he remained until 1898. He was also on the piano faculty of the Hamburg Conservatory from 1879 to 1887. He left a legacy of fine teaching pieces. Gurlitt died June 17, 1901, in his hometown of Altona.

# CONTENTS

Waltz ............................................. 4

Minuet ............................................. 5

A Sad Tale ......................................... 6

Mazurka ............................................ 7

In Spring .......................................... 8

Gavotte ............................................10

Through Forest and Field ..........................11

Spinning ..........................................12

Bright Is the Sky .................................13

The Music Box .....................................14

Flowing Stream ....................................15

Romance ...........................................16

Dancing ...........................................17

Festive Dance .....................................18

In the Garden .....................................20

Scherzo ...........................................21

The Storm .........................................22

# WALTZ
## Opus 187, No. 40

CORNELIUS GURLITT

**Moderato**

*p* *poco marcato il basso*

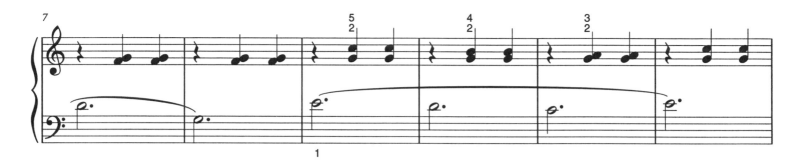

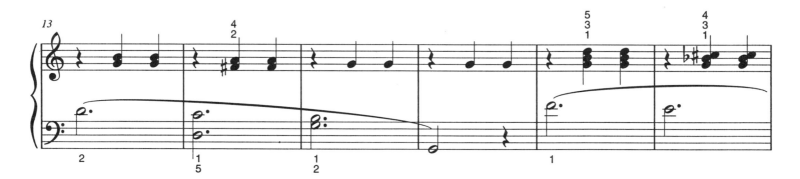

*dim.*

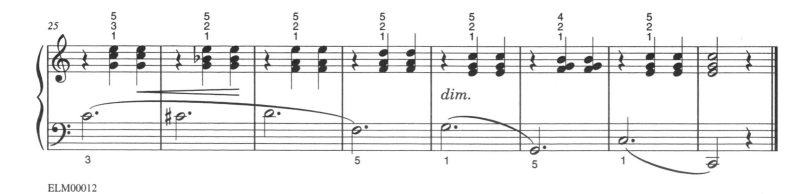

# MINUET

Opus 82, No. 34

# A SAD TALE

**Allegro non troppo**

# MAZURKA

### Opus 187, No. 47

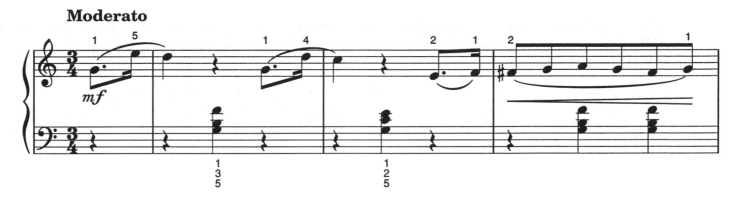

# IN SPRING

**Allegretto scherzando**

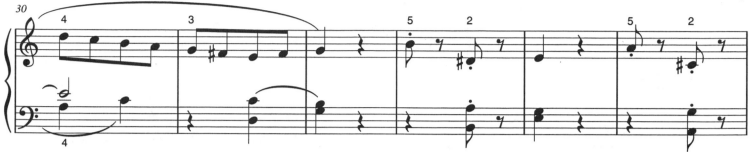

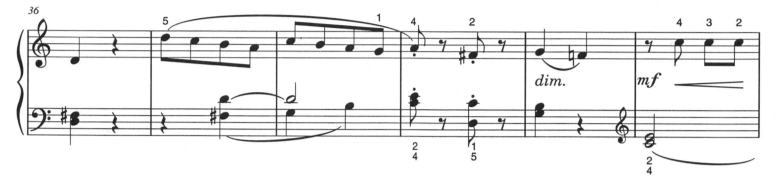

ELM00012

# GAVOTTE

# THROUGH FOREST AND FIELD

**Vivace**

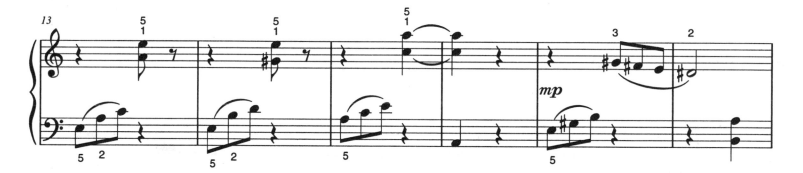

# SPINNING

Opus 141, No. 3

**Con moto**

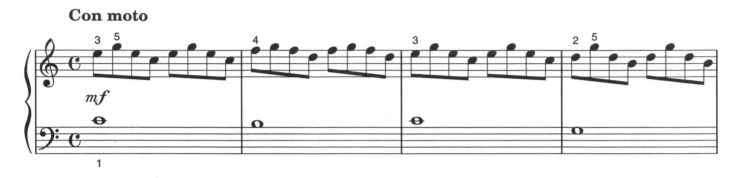

# BRIGHT IS THE SKY

Opus 140, No. 3

**Allegretto grazioso**

# THE MUSIC BOX

Opus 140, No. 8

**Allegretto**

# FLOWING STREAM

## Opus 141, No. 7

**Moderato**

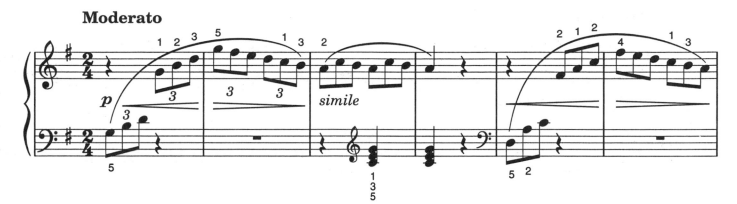

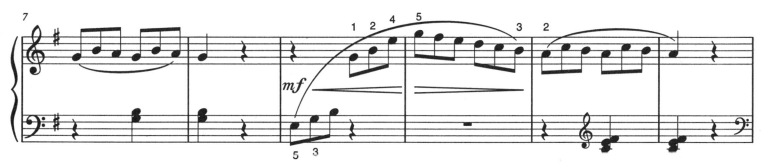

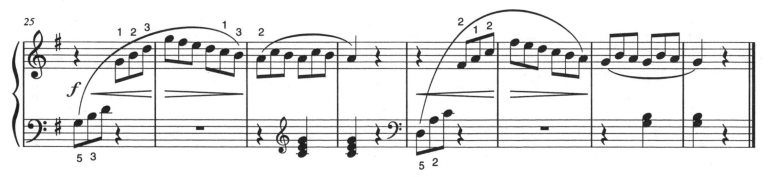

# ROMANCE

## Opus 141, No. 23

**Moderato**

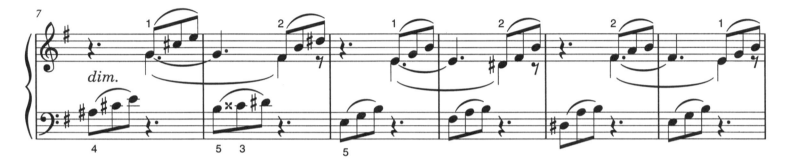

# DANCING
## Opus 141, No. 9

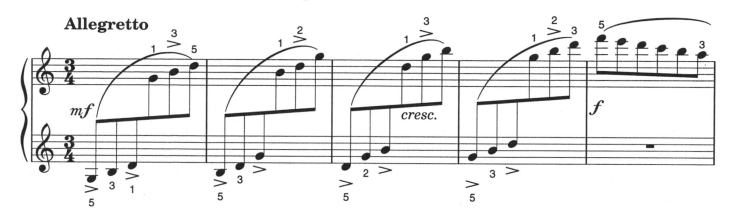

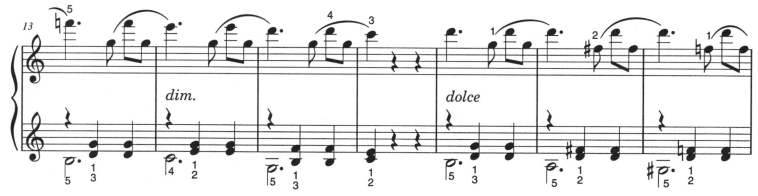

ELM00012

# A FESTIVE DANCE

## Opus 140, No. 7

**Tempo di valse**

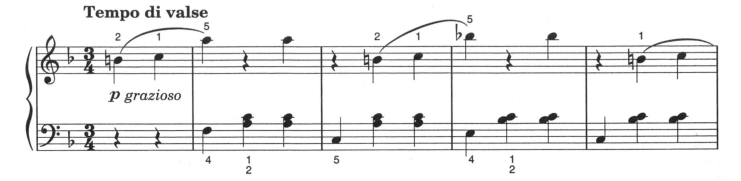

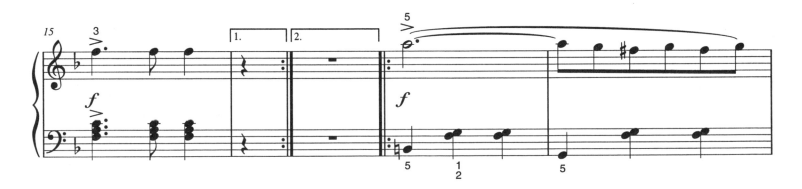

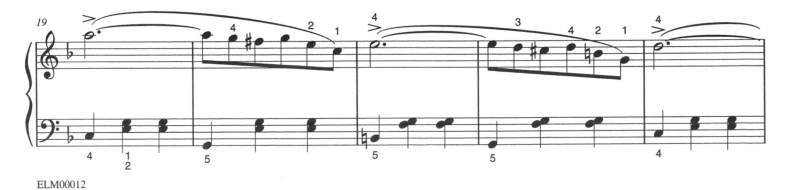

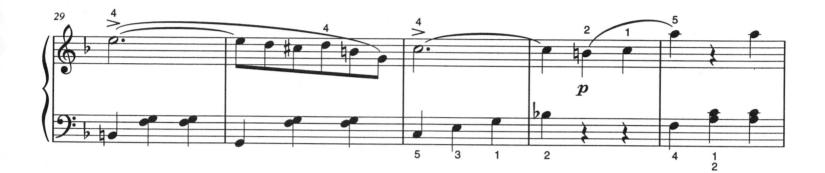

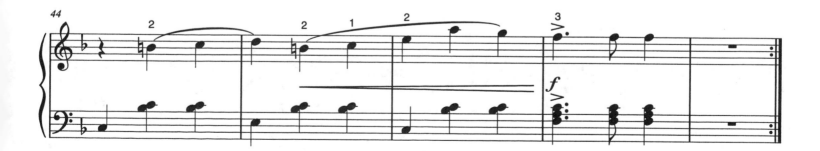

# IN THE GARDEN

Opus 82, No. 4

# SCHERZO

### Opus 140, No. 17

**Allegretto**

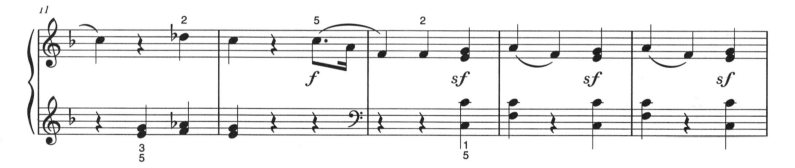

# THE STORM

## Opus 140, No. 20

**Molto vivace**

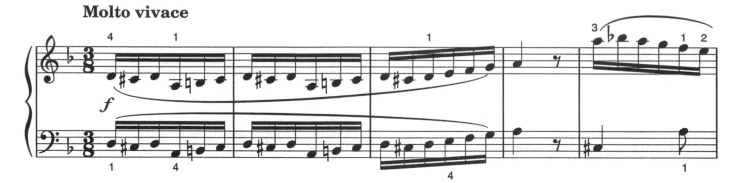

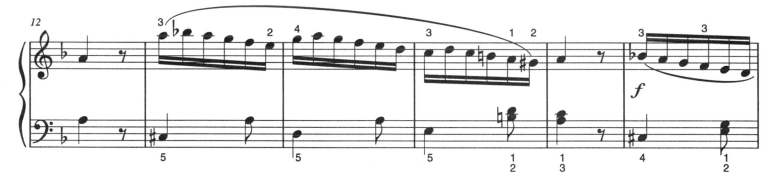

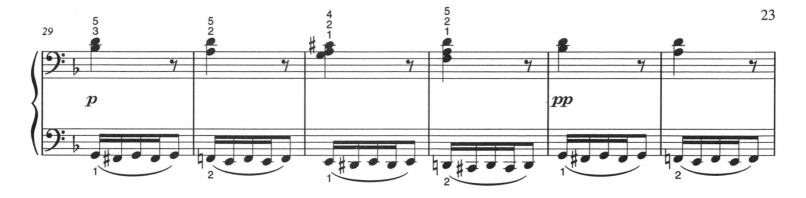

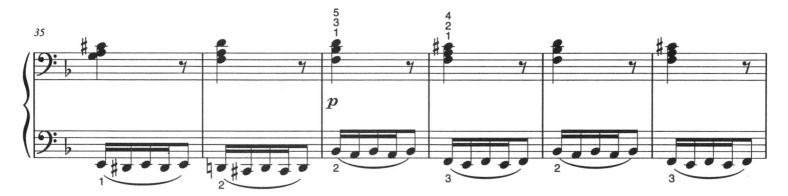

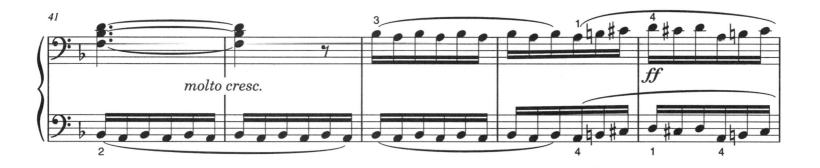

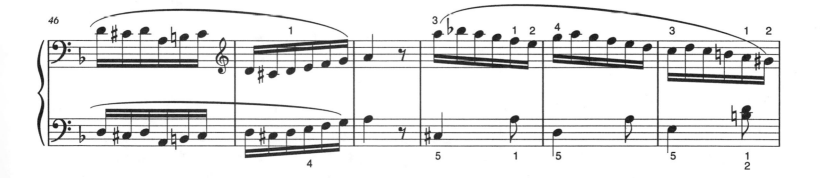

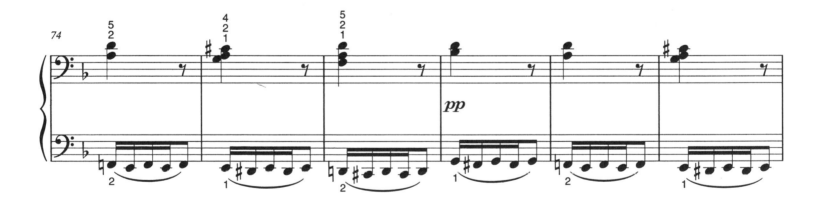